Minding My Own Business

AKA "Life", the real Fortune 500

CISLYN DEEN BROWN

Minding My Own Business

AKA "My Life" the real Fortune 500

By Cislyn Deen Brown

Cover art and all other art work by Alan Brown

Unless otherwise indicated, all scripture quotations are taken for the King James Version of the Bible

ISBN: 978-0-615-83973-8

FOR MORE INFORMATION CONTACT

Cislyn Brown
cislynbooks@yahoo.com
301.537.4764

Online ordering is available for all products

Dedication Page

This book is dedicated to my children Imraan Wise and Imtiyaz Wise. Thank you both for sharing this experience and being patient with me. Having been there, I want to alert you that there may be times when you will feel out of place and not sure where you fit in. May this book ignite in you a desire to become and remain aware that this life is precious and have values beyond that of a fortune 500 business. Therefore, you should monitor it, protect it, manage it, love it, cherish it and share it. In essence, it's your first business, so mind it.

FOREWORD

Presently, we are living in a world where many individuals live their lives leaving things up to chance. These persons go on their journey making no real life plans and having minimal focus or direction but as managers of our lives we should develop a strategic plan. A plan that encompasses all areas of our life and that will facilitate success. Cislyn Brown's book explains how the business of taking care of one's life is synonymous and evenly essential to that of managing a multi-billion-dollar corporation. This is why her attempt to sensitize and engage the world on this relevant topic through her book, *Minding My Own Business AKA "life", the real Fortune 500* is such a welcomed move in this era.

Indeed, the literary world is filled with myriad of work on self empowerment. However, *Minding My Own Business AKA "life", the real Fortune 500* is a unique two-part self empowerment tool that illustrates a distinctive and practical model for managing one's life. Brown explicitly establishes a step by step approach to using business strategies or standards in organizing and managing one's life, which can be easily understood by anyone. In my professional/vocational capacity, I am often times require to meet and counsel individuals who are struggling because they lack the self empowerment skills of managing their own lives. Therefore, I believe that everyone should be empowered with the knowledge and skills of defining his/her life. I usually have to assist these persons in creating some kind of self evaluation and self management for their lives.

Brown, in the first section of her book, encourages that the first step in the process of taking control of your life or "minding your own business" is to write down your mission statement and create long term and short-term goals that will enhance your ability to focus on your mission daily. She also shows how identifying and promoting one's strength, choosing the most suitable life partner, creating and consistently consulting a mission conscious team are just a few elements of the corporate model/framework that may be employed for personal life success. While the second half of the book is more engaging, allowing the reader to journalize his thoughts, feelings and ultimately his personal development as he works through the material.

It is the strength of Cislyn Brown's work that she so aptly compares and relates the treatment of a corporate business to that of personal life affairs. She sets forth clearly that the proper management of one's life is his/her paramount business. Out of her own personal experiences she was able to succinctly create this literary masterpiece; breaking through generational, gender and racial barriers.

I know of no other book that so carefully and thoroughly outlines the stages of employing the corporate models for personal or life enhancement. I am convinced that the principles delineated in this text will be of much help both the younger and more matured reader. I highly commend this book and pray that it will assist in producing a people whose desires have been ignited to become and remain aware that this "life is a precious gift from God that has values beyond that of a fortune 500 business". Thus, forcing readers to be good stewards of that which has be given to us. One should **monitor it, protect it, manage it, love it, cherish it and share it because it is your first business, so mind it**.

Dr. Jasmin Brown

Table of Contents

Introduction

Chapter 1   *12*
Mission statement

Chapter 2   *21*
General Business Description

Chapter 3   *35*
Operation Plan

Chapter 4   *39*
Board of Advisors

Chapter 5   *44*
Financial Plan

Chapter 6   *47*
The Conclusion of the whole matter

The Journaling Section   **53**

INTRODUCTION

According to the definition from Wikipedia, the free online encyclopedia, "**Mind your own business**" is a common English saying, which asks for a respect of other people's privacy. It can mean that a person should stop meddling in what does not concern that person, attend personal affairs of others instead of your own.

Over the years, we have all heard someone say "mind your business", "none of your business", "leave my business alone"; or my favorite, "I'm minding my own business and not attending to yours". In fact, we have become accustomed to interpreting these expressions as someone being a smart mouth or somewhat rude. We were taught indirectly that these expressions meant to bug off because this has nothing to do with us.

However, I have been enlightened with a new understanding regarding the phrase "mind your own business" and now understand it to be a reminder by others to take care of what's going on in my life and to mind it as if it is a business. People have been telling us this statement or we have been telling people the same for years; but, we have been brushing it off without any level of seriousness.

Therefore, the intent of this book is to serve as a relatable tool that will ignite the desire of seeking to manage one's own life in every department. Likewise, I hope this book motivates every reader to begin on a life changing and excited journey. One where he or she will become dedicated to overturn every stone in every corner of the world in search of the knowledge needed to live a fulfilled life.

Throughout this book, I will continuously provide standard approaches to operating a corporate business. I will then focus the reader's attention to the similarity of operating a business to that of operating one's own life. As such, I have taken the familiar portions of a business plan and standard organization manuals to serve as comparison to a person's life; thus, demonstrating that life is precious and indeed it is a business. It is a designer's original, one of kind and our job is to care for it as such.

So regardless of any atrocities, the past and current situations, this is our year in review. It is now time to observe our lives differently. This time, let's look at our life as a first-class business. So, with an attitude of total gratitude, come with me on a journey as we become aware, enlightened and inspired to manage our life with conscious intent as we would a great fortune 500 business.

Chapter 1

THE MISSION STATEMENT

Corporate Business

Traditionally, a mission statement is defined as a statement of the purpose of a company or an organization. In most cases, the mission statement is a clear and succinct representation of the organization's purpose for existence. Much time is often spent among an organization's executives ensuring that the mission statement really represents the company's morale position in 3 essential components:

1. *Key market – who is your target client/customer?*
2. *Contribution – what product or service do you provide to that client?*
3. *Distinction – what makes your product or service unique, so that the client would choose you?*

Life the Real Business

Similarly, to any good corporate business, our personal mission should be clearly defined, identified and/or discovered and should be the governing force that propels why we do what we do daily. In fact, my personal journey has taught me that finding and clarifying life's purpose will help us to move with greater focus and clarity every day of our life.

According to great teachers on this topic, our mission/purpose should push our goals, our ambition and our visions. If we think about it, we seek to become aware of the purpose of most things in life and utilize or rely on them accordingly. We know the purpose of the hand separate from that of the foot, the lungs separate from the heart, the microwave separate from the television, and the bank differently from the mortuary. In major societies, most things along with their purposes have been defined and societies as a collective whole are often cognizant of how to utilize them in order fulfill the various needs.

> "What a different story people would have to tell if they would adopt a definite purpose and stand by that ~~pose~~ until it had time to become an ~~a~~ ~~ming~~ purpose."
>
> **Napoleon Hill**
> *Laws of Success*

So, while my intent is not to give expert guidance on how to define your mission/purpose, I want to encourage every reader to seek after such transformative knowledge. I believe that unless you clearly define your purpose in your mind, you will most likely wander through life living according to the dreams others have for you; or, you will just fall into someone else's plan. In fact, I am convinced that life without purpose is like traveling without a destination in mind. More importantly, not only is it imperative to be knowledgeable of our mission/purpose, but we MUST become dedicated to living in FULL accordance with it.

WE ARE THE CEO OF OUR OWN LIFE

Corporate Business

The CEO and executive managers are the ones who are always most mindful of the organization mission/purpose for existing. They are always conscious of the greater purpose behind the day to day operations. In fact, in successful businesses, the CEO focuses on the mission and creates short term and long-term goals that will ensure that the mission is accomplished and/or represented.

Life the Real Business

It was during my struggles that it occurred to me that we are the CEO of our own life and we have full authority to define, discover and/or determine our mission. Like a corporate business, I will encourage you to write down your mission and create long term and short-term goals that will enhance your ability to focus on your mission daily. In fact, I will also recommend that it be written and displayed some place where it is quite visible and accessible.

During the process of defining my own mission, I discovered that defining and refining my own life's mission has helped to make it much easier to navigate through my personal stormy weathers. Each time that I fell off track, or felt overtaken by my trials, I was always drawn back to my mission. Here at this point, I was able to remind myself of why I had to find a way to fix whatever situation I was in. I was always driven to get back up and start again. A reminder of my mission always gave me a special recharge because I knew I wasn't finish as yet.

Make Your Mission Clear

When I got serious about accomplishing my life goals; and living according to my mission, I wrote them down. Additionally, I began to create vision boards that were symbolic of some of the goals that I wanted to accomplish in my life. I created step by step tasks to arrive at each goal. I must also emphasize that it is a great practice to review your mission each day before you begin your daily tasks. I find that this routine helps me to move more effectively and powerfully through the day. By frequently reminding yourself of your mission, you will become more focused and effective in every aspect of your life especially during times of making life changing decisions.

"Cherish your visions and your dreams as they are the children of your soul; the blue prints of your ultimate achievements."

- Napoleon Hill

The Bible states that Jesus declared His purpose f being on earth in several instances:

"I have come **that they may have life** and life m abundantly." (John 10:10b)

"[I have] come **to seek and to save that which w lost.**" (Luke 19:10)

Chapter 2

GENERAL BUSINESS DESCRIPTION

Corporate Business

Typically, an existing organization formally defines and establishes its description in a business plan and/or other official document. Here again, they focus on the mission, while expounding upon it with details within the following domains:

1. *Most Important Strengths and Core Competencies*
2. *Ownership status*
3. *Company History*
4. *Significant Challenges The Company Faces Now And In The Near Future*
5. *Long Term Plans For The Future*

Life the Real Business

When I was approaching my fortieth (40th) birthday, self - definition and self-description became very important to me. This was when I really began to assess my life. I started to engage myself in similar activities as that of a corporate organization.

I questioned myself repetitively:

a) What are the things that I know I am good at doing (regardless of what others thought)?

b) What are the things that I am passionate about?

c) What are the things that I do so intensely that time passes by without me noticing?

d) What have I accomplished in the forty years of being on earth?

e) What are the challenges that I encountered and what might have been the contributing factors?

f) What will I do to eliminate challenging encounters in the future?

g) Do I really want to legally unite with someone in the future?

h) What traits and characteristics are important to me in my partner?

i) What adjustments would I need to make to increase the probability of success should I unite with someone?

STRENGTHS AND CORE COMPETENCIES

<u>Corporate Business</u>

Understanding the organization's strength and core competencies is crucial in the organization's success. Therefore, corporate businesses frequently evaluate the factors that will make the company succeed and the major competitive strengths of the organization. They determine the company's potential for growth and or the manner in which to maintain stability. If companies plan for growth, they often have discussions of how it will be achieved. They often develop strategies for continued growth, increased production, diversification, and establish a time frame to accomplish the goal.

Life the Real Business

I have learned that it is most important to focus on our strengths even though we are aware of our barriers and/or weaknesses. There are so many of us with what I call 'suppressed strengths. In other words, there are a number of tasks that some of us perform well, which are overtly our strengths. However, we may have other hidden or undiscovered talents, gifts and/or passions that are yet to be uncovered. The fact that others may only be familiar with our overt strengths; unfortunately, these strengths are the ones that may get promoted.

Nevertheless, if we recognize all of who we are, and all of our strengths, then we will become conscious of all the cards we have to play with. No one knew of my passion to write. Therefore no one has ever encouraged me to write. In fact, singing is my overt talent and so everyone is anticipating that great step in me becoming the next Patti Labelle; who by the way is my vocal idol. I believe that it's not always about being discovered by someone; sometimes, it's about being discovered by SELF.

OWNERSHIP & LEGAL STATUS

Corporate Business

Corporate companies always clearly define their ownership status and are conscious of the benefit of such status. Nevertheless, a CEO knows that a company status may change at different times in its life span and will influence various benefits and responsibilities throughout its existence. Therefore, should a decision to change status is made; the pros and cons are always carefully evaluated. The most common statuses in a corporate business are sole proprietor, partnership, corporation, or limited liability corporation (LLC).

Furthermore, most business owners will take serious consideration before legally establishing business partnership with someone or another establishment. Usually, much effort is made to ensure that characteristics, values and/or business integrity complement each other. While each partner serves a specific purpose and has a role, ultimately the goal of collaborating is to fulfill the mission of the business and to ensure its growth and longevity.

Life the Real Business

While it is clear that corporate CEOs take exceptional consideration before making the decision to establish partnership and collaborating with their assets and business valuables; most of us often establish partnership, (wife, husband, girlfriend, boyfriend) based on shallow emotional and impulsive reasons. Many times, when we consider merging or joining our lives with another, we are afraid to ask the right questions because we don't want to be judged. My real point is that our life is so valuable and the decisions we make often have long term implications on us and often the ones closest to us. Therefore, it behooves us to be exceptionally cautious and consider the depth and full implications of exposing and sharing our values, our assets, our family, in general our LIFE BUSINESS with someone else at any level.

CONSIDER THE FOLLOWING QUESTIONS:

✓ What does our partner say about us?

✓ How does he/she reflect and/or complement our mission?

✓ What purpose does he/she serve or what role does he/she fulfill in our personal operation?

✓ How efficient is our partner in functioning within the identified role?

The only way to adequately answer these questions is to revert to the beginning where we declared our mission. Then and only then will we understand that like a successful corporate business, choosing a partner that contradicts our mission will sabotage growth and ultimately impedes longevity of our God given establishment.

So often we try to get a gallon of fluid out of a quart container then we become frustrated. In fact, if we reflect on most failed relationships, we will see that all the evidence were present in the initial stage of the relationship highlighting the incompatibilities. If we ask ourselves all the right questions we will hear the answers in our hearts. Nevertheless, it's never too late to adjust; therefore, if we are in a situation that seems troublesome, by all means we should do everything in our power to fix ourselves and move forward with purpose.

KNOW YOUR OWN CORE VALUES

Consider this, if you significantly value tertiary education; yet, you are in a committed relationship with someone who places little or no value on

> *Unequal Yoke, the dysfunctions followed by the inevitable pain and agony of time wasted*
>
> - *Cislyn Deen Brown*

education. This individual's lack or scant regard for higher education may even be projected in his/her opposition against the process of securing tertiary education (e.g. disapproves loans etc). What then can be foreseen in the future of this relationship? The responses may vary including: fights about money, someone giving up on his/her dream, resentment or ultimate dissolution of the relationship. The problem is how many things would have transpired during this major conflict and who or what would have gotten caught in this crossfire?

> **Unequal Yoke, the dysfunctions followed by the inevitable pain and agony of time wasted.**

Consider again if we significantly valued prestigious lifestyle; yet, we are in a committed relationship with someone who didn't care if they were living in a sardine pan. What can be foreseen in the future of this relationship? Again, someone may answer fights about money, someone giving up his/her dream, resentment or ultimate dissolution of the relationship. The same question is how many things would have transpired during this major conflict and who or what would have gotten caught in this crossfire? *Unequal Yoke, the dysfunctions followed by the inevitable pain and agony of time wasted.* No one knows what the future may bring. Nevertheless, it seems incredibly beneficial to make decisions that will ultimately support our mission and enhance our growth and longevity.

Corporate Business

Routinely, organizations review their successes, events that affected success as they review the amount of years in business, failures and lessons learned. Likewise, managers review and discuss significant past problems along with ways of identifying the solutions. In some industries, such as the human service field that I have worked for over 20 years, the CEO and other executive managers would present analytical data of the organization's overall status and performance to the Board of Directors at least on a quarterly basis.

Life the Real Business

I have often reflected on my entire life, contemplating all the mistakes, perceived failures along with the contributing factors that I had encountered on my journey. These reviews were often very painful. I am now convinced that this pain was invoked because of the feelings of being forced to make tough decisions based on exposed suppressed personal truth. I often thought to myself how could I

> *If I consciously repeat the same behaviors that gave me unwanted outcomes then how conscious am I really?*
>
> - Cislyn D. Brown

know what contributed to my failures and still continued to exhibit those same behaviors? What does that make me?

So, as I rolled back the curtains of memory, and reviewed my own life, I had to admit that I had been living in a space that contradicted the mission and goals that I have established for myself. It was then that I decided to make several drastic decisions and live my life according to my own truth. Additionally, I became more passionate about completing this book to serve as my personal reminder to focus intensely on my own life mission.

Now, that was how this process affected me. However, I am quite aware that everyone will have his/her own experience. Each reader's experience may be totally different; nevertheless, the point of it all is that this experience should ignite the process of self–examination. It should also stimulate growth and/or confirm that we are on the correct path; hence, we ought to take much effort in securing where we are or what we have.

Again, as conscious people who are in control of our own life, at some point we have to look at our successes so as to repeat or duplicate the behaviors that contributed to those accomplishments. Quite importantly, we need to also analyze our failures in order to learn and develop new strategies that will effectively assist us in avoiding or minimizing the occurrences that do not serve us well.

REPUTATION MATTERS

Corporate Business

Most established and renowned organizations are exceptionally mindful of their reputation in the community. There is always the question of whether or not their reputation represents the organization's philosophies and core principles. Small, yet profoundly significant steps are taken to create and define a clear physical image, logo, slogan and common operation practices that serve as reminder or affirmation of the company's mission.

Life the Real Business

I am aware that some people may say they don't care about what anyone thinks about them. However, let's ask ourselves the following questions to examine whether or not we have created the reputation that we so desire via our communication, behaviors, actions, verbal expressions and outward appearance:

1. **Am I trust worthy?**
2. **Am I truthful to my own mission?**
3. **Do I have integrity?**
4. **Do I reflect my core values?**
5. **Does my life represent my definition of self?**

A person may have the most profound message to deliver that could save millions of lives. Nevertheless, if the impact of the message is being deflected by undesired reputation which demolishes the message, that's a big problem. It is at this point where I will suggest that you ask yourself what you value more. It may be that you are the most knowledgeable person on cultural history, spiritual awareness, or even financial enrichment; however, if you are perceived as an untrustworthy, lacking integrity, hostile or as a person who has bad mental attitude; chances are, not too many people will want to hear your life changing message. Subsequently, it is our reputation that will separate us from others who may appear to have similar mission. Thus, our goal should be for others to view us the way we view ourselves; as well as, to be mindful to represent ourselves as we defined ourselves. Overall, as CEO, you can define and describe yourself. Again, it's your life and you can live it anyway that you choose. Once you know your mission/purpose and create a definition of self that represents and serves as affirmation of self, do not contradict your own self. Living a life that contradicts your mission/purpose will only lead to ill-health, stagnation and frustration throughout your life.

Chapter 3

OPERATIONAL PLAN

Corporate Business

An operation plan directly describes the organization missions and goals, program objectives, and program activities. It is a subset of strategic work plan that describes short-term approaches for achieving milestones. It also explains how, or what portion of a strategic plan will be put into operation during a given operational period or a given budgetary term. Ultimately, there are four main questions that an operational plan address. These four questions will become our focus as we review our life business in this chapter.

1. Where are we now?
2. Where do we want to be?
3. How do we get there?
4. How do we measure our progress?

Life the Real Business

By now, it should have become clear to all my readers the thought process that I am attempting to invoke. As we read the corporate definition in each section, our minds should immediately start reflecting on how we may begin to apply these corporate models to our personal lives.

So, as we make the mental comparison, I want us to look at five questions (unlike four in a corporate business) to use to analyze our personal operational plan:

1. Where are we now?
2. How is it working for us?
3. Where do we want to be?
4. How do we get there?
5. How do we measure our progress?

Many of us on our life journey may find ourselves riding in a repetitive and safe mode. Again, if we haven't determined our mission, this may just be the unfulfilling place we will find ourselves in life. Maybe, you are a person who is already cognizant of your mission. It might even be the case that you have been aware of this knowledge for a while. Nonetheless, it is imperative to do self-examination in order to move beyond the knowledge of the mission and into its activation.

Too often we just play it by air as if we really have no control over the things as they occur. But clearly as the CEO of our own operation, after coming into this state of awareness, one thing is required and that is decisions must be made. As the CEO, our decisions will be based on our

"First comes thought...Then organization of that thought into ideas and plans. Then transformation of those plans into reality. The beginning as you'll observe, is your imagination"

- Napoleon Hill

mission and overall long term and short-term objectives. Therefore, performing inventory will force us to evaluate how well the decisions we make are serving us and supporting our mission and aiding to propel us in the direction of our ultimate long- and short-term objectives. So, regardless of our situation, or where we find our self on our personal journey, if we are operating our life as a business, we must at some point stop and look at where we are presently and where we want or plan to be in the future. In order to make this successful transition, like a good corporate business, we have to find a strategy that's proven and effective. Then we must make the conscious decision and move into the implementation mode to change our state and change our story.

I remember when I was a freshman in college; the president said one thing that replays in my mind often. He said four years will come whether we graduate or not. As I have gotten older and have been going through this process of "minding my own business", I have been reflecting on this statement more and more. I now live in a state of consciousness that five years, ten years or even retirement will come whether I create a plan and work it or not.

Chapter 4

Professional and Advisory Support

Corporate Business

An Advisory team is usually selected for its knowledge and experience and typically serves the purpose of making recommendations to the organizational body. Executive leaders rely on their advisory team to provide constructive feedback and to assist and serve as an advocate, supporter, and resource for the president or CEO.

There are numerous benefits of creating an advisory team. Benefits include the diversity of opinion and the experience it can bring to facilitate an improvement in the leadership of a company. Additionally, an advisory team may be beneficial in that it can provide the organization with business development opportunities, strategy development, and having an outside perspective.

Life the Real Business

We cannot know it all or rely only on self. As the leader of your own life, it is important to understand what purpose each person serves and interact with them accordingly. Everyone has a role; but, often we become frustrated with our partners, friends or family because we are misusing or simply just have unrealistic expectations of them. For instance, we all know that we rely on our lawyer for legal advice and not for emotional or financial services.

Create a Mission Conscious Team

We all have heard that we are what we eat. I like to believe this concept applies to what we consume, physically, socially, intellectually, emotionally and spiritually as well. Therefore, as it pertains to our lives, we should begin to review the pool of people that are in our circle; as well as, the quality of information that we absorb in our minds and our hearts. At this stage in our lives, this is what will begin to either confirm the old tapes from our past or erase

40

them. For example, if we know without a doubt that we want to pursue being an entrepreneur, while on the contrary, all of our friends barely want a job. Yet, these are the people we hang with and talk to every day. We may even try to share our dreams and aspirations with them, because that's what we do with our friends. However, the chance of getting the needed support and encouragement is slim to none.

There are some friends in our lives that are great to hang out with, have a great laugh, party with and have the best time. But so often I find that we may feel compel to carry all our friends everywhere we go in life. For example, God may bless us with a corporate business or break through opportunity and we feel obligated to force-fit our hanging friends or spouse in this new setting/situation. In these instances, we often experience self-induced hardship because there we have created new expectations within their new role while in most cases that was not the basis of the relationship to begin with.

This is where we look at our mission, how we described ourselves, consider where we are and where we are going, then look at our friends, mates and confidants and see how they reflect us or where do they fit in. We should then consider how they will contribute or detract, propel or restrain, support or suffocate us in achieving and/or fulfilling our goals. This is where we begin to ask some of the following questions:

A. Who do you go to for advice?
B. What type of books do you read?
C. Who can you run to for support?
D. Who do you go to for expert recommendation for legal, financial, relationship, educational, emotional matters?
E. Who do you talk to when you are about to make a life changing decision?
F. Who do you talk to if you think you made a mistake?
G. What type of music do you listen to?
H. How do you feed your spiritual self
I. How do you rejuvenate the mind?

No one can make it alone and even the strong needs to be sustained. Hence, surrounding ourselves with like-minded people or knowing where to go for the professional, spiritual and/or emotional support that we will need is absolutely critical. In the same way that we perform inventory on our own accomplishments and

42

milestone on this journey, it is imperative that we perform inventory on our friends and circle of influence. We must begin to critically analyze how much value we place on people and things such as, books we read, speakers we listen to, songs we dance to and in general what we surround ourselves with every day.

Chapter 5

FINANCIAL PLAN & STABILITY

Corporate Business

Within a business plan, the financial plan comprises of profit and loss projection, a cash-flow projection, a projected balance sheet, and a breakeven calculation. A company can use the financial plan to predict the financial future of a company. More important, the process of thinking through the financial plan often improves the company's insight into the inner financial workings of the company.

Life the Real Business

While I am not the Suze Orman of finance, as I became obedient on my journey I developed a deeper and deeper consciousness of the significance of financial awareness. I am now convinced that unless we mind this aspect of our life, we will become overwhelmed by financial turmoil. Therefore, the intent of this chapter is to increase awareness, as in previous chapters, and serve as a reminder that we must control every area of this precious business (our life); because, any area left unmanaged will cause trouble for the other well-maintained areas.

Everything that I have read has led me to believe that a financial plan creates financial stability, which is one of the most common dreams people have. People aspire career advancement for a better pay, some engage in business, while some invest. No matter what path we choose to travel, we all hope it will lead to one thing, to earn more in order to become financially secured, live and enjoy a comfortable life.

So, let us go back to the beginning to where we define our purpose, our description, and then our operation plan and connect the dots with a clear financial plan. This connection will give a well-defined idea of what lifestyle we want to live, where we want to live, what we want to accomplish and how much finance we would need in order to do so. Don't get me wrong, this plan can change at any time. In fact, as we project the future of our business (life or corporate), being financially conscious can be a great motivator and inspiration to guide us in planning, implementing and making the necessary adjustments needed on our journey to move into full manifestation of our life desires.

To have a financial plan means our money will go where it was intended to go and do that which ultimately translates into our money covering a multitude of scenarios and making money work on our behalf. It means we are being prepared for whatever may come; thus, allowing us to focus on the other areas of our life. Most people fail to see the good things of becoming financially stable and just desire to be rich. However, being rich is merely having the money and material possessions. But, without a plan we will not know how to properly orchestrate and utilize our money to create financial longevity.

Chapter 6

THE CONCLUSION OF THE WHOLE MATTER

Whether or not I have gone over every aspect of operating a corporate business, the objective of this book is to increase awareness that like a corporate business, our lives have departments that require special attention, monitoring and supervision. Since we are the CEO of our own lives, we are responsible for taking charge and putting the pieces together or finding qualified people who are able to assist us in putting them together.

Now that we have considered some major aspects of operating life as a business, we now see how it all ties together. We see that as a CEO everything centers on the original purpose and or the mission that the organization has given itself. So in essence, being untrue to your own mission is the biggest disservice to self EVER. This is our life, we all have the opportunity to live it anyway we choose. The question is how will we choose to live it.

I have read the Bible, the Quran and many religious books. In them, I read about the great people and prophets that preceded us and their different gifts, talents, authority, powers and/or things that made them memorable. Moses divided the Red Sea, David slew Goliath, Jesus turned water into wine and there are many more examples that I could use for reference. However, I often wondered about Adam, the first man. I wondered what was his great gift, talent or special power. I've concluded that his ultimate power was the POWER OF CHOICE.

We may not be able to part the Red Sea, turn water into wine or raise people from the dead; but, we all can make choices every day about our own life. So knowing our purpose/mission and clearly making a choice to define ourselves any way we so desire and living accordingly is crucial to minding this precious gift, **LIFE, OUR OWN BUSINESS.**

I have heard it repetitively, live according to your mission; and if you don't know what your mission is, then discovering your mission automatically becomes your mission. Once we become knowledgeable of our mission, we should define ourselves and represent ourselves accordingly.

Macy's never wants their customers to ever mistake them for Kmart whenever they look at the building, walk in their stores; or even more so, whenever they use their products. Nordstrom always want us to have a Nordstrom experience when they serve us while Subway always wants us to have a *"eat fresh"* experience. Then how different are we? We should take the same level of pride and caution to ensure that we represent ourselves according to our own definition at all times. Each day is critical in our operation and should be taken seriously. Every decision we make about our life affects every aspect of it. It's our business, we should mind it.

Here are some tips to help you as you begin your journey of *Minding Your Own Business*:

1) Understand you mission/purpose

2) Know what makes you distinct from the rest

3) Write down your mission and read often

4) Write your own description of yourself

5) Anything you don't like about yourself, change it

6) live according to your own description that will make your life business credible

7) Determine, control and maintain financial soundness

8) Read and study all the great people you admire

9) Pick and keep friends that reflect you

10) Pick and keep spouse that reflects you

11) Do inventory of your life OFTEN

12) Have a plan for your life

13) Be mindful with whom you share your plan

14) WORK YOUR PLAN & allow your plan to work for you

I have learned the following lessons the hard way:

> Non-expert people will have a lot of advice for your life, if you follow them blindly and fail, they will never take the blame.

> If you allow them, people will stand on your eyelid to reach where they are going.

> If you don't know who you are and or do not trust yourself enough, people will see your potential and use it to serve ONLY their plan.

> If you don't know your worth, then you won't know what to ask for, thus, people will put any tag on you that serves them ONLY.

> Loving self is not equivalent to being selfish.

> You must believe in yourself even if you are the only one that does.

> If you don't define yourself and know your purpose, then people will define you and convince you that's who you are.

So I say this, know yourself and to *thine own-self be true*. If you fall, get back up and start again and again and again until they say "ashes to ashes and dust to dust". If you don't know where to start, ask and the answer will be given; seek and you will find; knock and many doors will be open onto you as it has for many others. God bless you and guide you on your path. I pray for abundance and prosperity, true awareness and consciousness of self and that this will set you on your way to search every corner of the world until you discover your truth.

THANK YOU FOR READING

THE JOURNALING SECTION

OVERVIEW & GUIDELINES

Congratulations on completing "Minding My Own Business". I hope that you are excited about your next chapter as I am. I have created this section to assist you in moving into implementation mode on your journey of minding your own business. This is a hands-on approach of taking journaling to another level. It's also an approach that will allow you to record your self-assessment in various domains and monitor your progress periodically.

Write in this section and update as you go. It will become interesting to go back and review years from now and see how far we have come (or not). Again, my goal is to stimulate you into becoming so focus on your own life that you won't have time to become caught up in the distractions around you.

INSTRUCTIONS:

1. *Answer each question as honestly as possible.*

2. *Once you have realized that there is an area that requires change, write it down on the goal sheet on the long term objective line.*

3. *Next, write down at least three steps that you will take to accomplish the long term goal.*

4. *Being measurable means you should indicate quantitative values. For example, I will walk three days per week for 30 minutes for 30 consecutive weeks; or, I will walk two miles daily three days per week for ten consecutive weeks etc. Have fun with this.*

5. *Next, think about the support or advantages you have accessible that will enhance the possibility of achieving this goal*

6. *Finally, think about what obstacles that may hinder accomplishing this goal*

MY MISSION STATEMENT

To the best of your ability, write down what you believe to be your ultimate purpose for being here. Think about your passion, what drives you, when do you FEEL most gratified? Use your own words.

GOAL SHEET

DESIRED LONG -TERM GOAL:

SHORT TERM GOALS/METHODOLOGY (*Must be Measurable*)

TARGET DATE:

ACCESSIBLE SUPPORT:

BARRIERS TO ATTAINING GOAL:

GOAL SHEET

DESIRED LONG -TERM GOAL:

SHORT TERM GOALS/METHODOLOGY (*Must be Measurable*)

TARGET DATE:

ACCESSIBLE SUPPORT:

BARRIERS TO ATTAINING GOAL:

In most cases we can distinguish the differences between one organization from the next. This is true even down to the exterior, logo, slogans, colors, design etc. For example, if someone should take you to McDonalds and the word McDonalds was not written on the building, could you tell that you were at McDonalds? The answer is yes. You would recognize the consistent menu, colors, logo etc. If you walked inside Macy's without seeing the word Macy's what are some dead giveaway that you are inside Macy's and not Target or the reverse?

The following questions are intended to do several things. They are intended to probe you to start being conscious about your own self-description and how our actual lives parallel these descriptions or not. Additionally, they are intended to probe us to begin to create an action plan to either maintain this life or begin to create the life that our hearts desire.

Likewise, they are intended to examine the inner depth of our self and determine if this is our life or the life others have convinced us to be ours. Feel free to add as many more questions that may not be listed. Remember, this is an exercise to stimulate our minds to become aware and live aware. I believe that if we can't define and describe ourselves, then once again we are at the mercy of someone to impose their description of us on us. In time we may begin to believe those descriptions and how self destructive those descriptions may be if they are inaccurate.

Additionally, I want us to really consider if we have legitimate reasons to hold on to some of the things we think that we love. If living in a bad neighborhood is your current situation, but it allows you to save money and you are actually saving with a plan to relocate is different from just living there, hating it without a plan to move. If you really love your hair short; but, you are currently wearing your hair long how is that serving you? Ultimately, there are numerous questions that we can ask ourselves. Therefore, as long as we are asking questions for the purpose of self-examination and self-inventory, then we are on the right track.

MY COLORS:

1) What is/are my current favorite color/s?

    _____

2) What are the benefits and /or how is this working
   for me?

    _____

    _____

    _____

    _____

3) How is this evident in my life?

    _____

    _____

    _____

    _____

4) What is my desired/preferred color?

    _____

5) What is my action plan to maintain or obtain
   what I truly desire?

    _____

    _____

    _____

MY ATTIRE

1) What is my current and routine fashion style?
   _____
   _____
   _____
   _____

2) What are the benefits and /or how is this working for me?
   _____
   _____
   _____
   _____

3) How is this evident in my life?
   _____
   _____
   _____

4) What is my desired fashion style?
   _____
   _____
   _____

5) What is my action plan to maintain or obtain what I truly desire? _____
   _____
   _____
   _____

MY PHYSICAL PHYSIC:

1) What's my current weight and/or measurements?

    _____

    _____

2) What are the benefits and /or how is this working for me?

    _____

    _____

    _____

    _____

3) How is this evident in my life?

    _____

    _____

    _____

    _____

4) What is my desired weight and/or measurements?

    _____

    _____

    _____

    _____

5) What is my action plan to maintain or obtain what I truly desire?

    _____

    _____

    _____

MY INTERNAL HEALTH:

1) What's my current health profile, (weight, blood pressure, cholesterol, blood sugar levels etc.?

_____
_____
_____
_____

2) What are the benefits and /or how is this working for me?

_____
_____
_____
_____

3) How is this evident in my life?

_____
_____
_____
_____

4) What is my action plan to maintain or obtain what I truly desire?

_____
_____
_____
_____

MY HAIR

1) What is my current hair style or status (color, length, texture, style etc.)?

_____

_____

_____

_____

2) What are the benefits and /or how is this working for me?

_____

_____

_____

_____

3) How is this evident in my life?

_____

_____

_____

4) What is my desired hair style or status (color, length, texture, style etc.)?

_____

_____

_____

5) What is my action plan to maintain or obtain what I truly desire (color, length, texture etc)?

_____

_____

_____

RELATIONSHIP

1) What is my current relationship status?

_____

_____

_____

2) What are the benefits and /or how is this working for me?

_____

_____

_____

_____

3) How is this evident in my life?

_____

_____

_____

_____

4) What is my desired Status?

_____

_____

5) What is my action plan to maintain or obtain what I truly desire?

_____

_____

_____

_____

MY HABITS

1) What behavior/s or ritual/s do I repeat daily, weekly monthly, or annually consistently?

_____

_____

_____

_____

2) What are the benefits and /or how is this working for me?

_____

_____

3) How is this evident in my life?

_____

_____

_____

4) What behavior/s or ritual/s do I DESIRE to repeat daily, weekly monthly, or annually consistently?

_____

_____

_____

_____

5) What is my action plan to maintain or obtain what I truly desire?

_____

_____

_____

_____

MY SPIRITUALITY

1. What is/are my current method of spirituality practice/s?

   _____

   _____

   _____

   _____

2. What are the benefits and /or how is this working for me?

   _____

   _____

   _____

3. How is this evident in my life?

   _____

   _____

   _____

   _____

4. What is my desired method of spirituality practices/s?

   _____

   _____

   _____

5. What is my action plan to maintain or obtain what I truly desire?

   _____

   _____

ENTERTAINMENT

1) What type of music/s do I listen to; what do I watch on TV and how often?

_____

_____

_____

_____

2) What are the benefits and /or how is this working for me?

_____

_____

_____

_____

3) How is this evident in my life?

_____

_____

_____

4) What is my desired music, TV show and frequency?

_____

_____

_____

_____

5) What is my action plan to maintain or obtain what I truly desire?

_____

_____

1) What books do I currently read or have read and how often?

_____

_____

_____

_____

2) What are the benefits and /or how is this working for me?

_____

_____

_____

3) How is this evident in my life?

_____

_____

_____

4) What books do I desire to read and how often?

_____

_____

_____

_____

5) What is my action plan to maintain or obtain what I truly desire?

_____

_____

_____

SOCIAL RECREATION

1. What do I currently do for fun; how do I unstressed or spend my free time?

   _____

   _____

   _____

   _____

2. What are the benefits and /or how is this working for me?

   _____

   _____

   _____

3. How is this evident in my life?

   _____

   _____

   _____

4. What places have I traveled outside of my current town?

   _____

   _____

   _____

5. What places have I traveled outside of my current state?

   _____

   _____

   _____

6. What places have I traveled outside of my current country?

_____

_____

_____

_____

7. What do I really desired to do for fun/s?

_____

_____

_____

_____

8. Where are the places I desire to travel?

_____

_____

_____

_____

9. What is my action plan to maintain or obtain what I truly desire?

_____

_____

_____

_____

_____

_____

_____

<u>What are some Things I absolutely must have</u>: (Don't want to live without)?

_____

_____

_____

_____

<u>What are some Things I don't like</u>: (Conditions to avoid, what sets me off?)

_____

_____

_____

_____

<u>What are some Things I am good at</u>: (even if no one else thinks I'm good at it):

_____

_____

_____

_____

_____

GOAL SHEET

DESIRED LONG -TERM GOAL:

SHORT TERM GOALS/METHODOLOGY (*Must be Measurable*)

TARGET DATE:

ACCESSIBLE SUPPORT:

BARRIERS TO ATTAINING GOAL:

GOAL SHEET

DESIRED LONG -TERM GOAL:

SHORT TERM GOALS/METHODOLOGY (*Must be Measurable*)

TARGET DATE:

ACCESSIBLE SUPPORT:

BARRIERS TO ATTAINING GOAL:

NEIGHBORHOOD

1) Describe my current environment?

_____

_____

_____

2) What are the benefits and /or how is this working for me?

_____

_____

_____

3) How is this evident in my life?

_____

_____

_____

4) What is my desired environment?

_____

_____

_____

5) What is my action plan to maintain or obtain what I truly desire?

_____

_____

_____

MY HOME

1) What is my current status and home type (own, rent, boarding, other)?

_____

_____

2) What are the benefits and /or how is this working for me?

_____

_____

_____

3) How is this evident in my life?

_____

_____

_____

4) What is my desired status and home type?

_____

_____

_____

5) What is my action plan to maintain or obtain what I truly desire?

_____

_____

_____

_____

MY ASSETS

1) What are my current possessions?

_____

_____

_____

_____

2) What are the benefits and /or how is this working for me?

_____

_____

_____

_____

3) How is this evident in my life?

_____

_____

_____

4) What is my desired possession/s?

_____

_____

_____

5) What is my action plan to maintain or obtain what I truly desire?

_____

_____

_____

_____

MY METHOD OF TRANSPORTATION

1) How do I commute daily?

_____

_____

_____

2) What are the benefits and /or how is this working for me?

_____

_____

_____

3) How is this evident in my life?

_____

_____

_____

_____

4) What is my desired preference/s?

_____

_____

_____

5) What is my action plan to maintain or obtain what I truly desire?

_____

_____

_____

_____

CAREER PATH

1) What is my current occupational status?

_____

_____

_____

_____

2) What are the benefits and /or how is this working for me?

_____

_____

_____

_____

3) How is this evident in my life?

_____

_____

_____

_____

4) What is my desired preference?

_____

_____

_____

5) What is my action plan to maintain or obtain what I truly desire?

_____

_____

_____

_____

1) What is my highest academic achievement?

_____

_____

_____

_____

2) What are the benefits and /or how is this working for me?

_____

_____

_____

3) How is this evident in my life?

_____

_____

_____

4) What is my desired academic achievement?

_____

_____

_____

_____

5) What is my action plan to maintain or obtain what I truly desire?

_____

_____

_____

_____

FINANCE:

1) What is my current level of financial stability (saving funds, emergency funds, retirement etc)?

_____

_____

_____

2) What are the benefits and /or how is this working for me?

_____

_____

_____

3) How is this evident in my life?

_____

_____

_____

4) What is my desired status?

_____

_____

_____

_____

5) What is my action plan to maintain or obtain what I truly desire?

_____

_____

_____

_____

GOAL SHEET

DESIRED LONG -TERM GOAL:

SHORT TERM GOALS/METHODOLOGY (*Must be Measurable*)

TARGET DATE:

ACCESSIBLE SUPPORT:

BARRIERS TO ATTAINING GOAL:

GOAL SHEET

DESIRED LONG -TERM GOAL:

SHORT TERM GOALS/METHODOLOGY (*Must be Measurable***)**

TARGET DATE:

ACCESSIBLE SUPPORT:

BARRIERS TO ATTAINING GOAL:

PROFESSIONAL AND ADVISORY SUPPORT

	NAME	ROLE	Effectiveness)
ACQUAINTANCES			
Best Friend			
Friend 2			
Friend 3			
Emergency Contact			
Mentor			
PROFESSIONAL SUPPORT			
PCP			
Dentist			
Attorney			
Financial advisor			
Spiritual Leader			
Counselor			
Casual Friend/s			
Family Support			
Books I Read			

PROFESSIONAL AND ADVISORY SUPPORT

	NAME	ROLE	Effectiveness)
SOCIAL GROUP			
MEMBERSHIP			
ADDITIONAL SUPPORT			

GOAL SHEET

DESIRED LONG -TERM GOAL:

SHORT TERM GOALS/METHODOLOGY (*Must be Measurable*)

TARGET DATE:

ACCESSIBLE SUPPORT:

BARRIERS TO ATTAINING GOAL:

GOAL SHEET

DESIRED LONG -TERM GOAL:

SHORT TERM GOALS/METHODOLOGY (*Must be Measurable*)

TARGET DATE:

ACCESSIBLE SUPPORT:

BARRIERS TO ATTAINING GOAL:

ACKNOWLEDGEMENTS

How do I say thanks for all the things that God has done? While I do not have the words to express my eternal gratitude, I am fully conscious of the fact that all that I am or ever hope to become is because of His abundant provision and outpour of His unending mercy.

To my parents who made the ultimate sacrifice, I thank you without end. **DADDY** Rest in Peace, you protected me and with your stern reprimands and such incomprehensible love you taught me self-love and unique worthiness. As a young girl, you told me repeatedly that I was "comely". Strangely enough, I didn't know what that word meant or understood what you were saying. Yet, during the times when I struggled most with my image and worth, I often heard your voice resonating in my ears over and over that I am "comely". At those moments, my spirit was always revived because of that soothing love that overfilled my heart because **DADDY SAID** I am comely. Now I know that you had chosen a unique word, for that time, to impress upon me that I am unique and beautiful. Thank you.

MOM, I often wondered if I were adopted because I could never understand how I could have been born to someone so calm, kind, nice, loving, God-fearing, and with such perseverance. I often dreamt of growing up and having those same qualities but in reality, I knew that I had such a long way to go. Thank you

To my children, Imraan and Imtiyaz Wise, I am always so thankful for having you both. I prayed for great children and God exceeded my expectations and blessed me with you both. How awesome is our Lord? I look at you both and I am reminded of the endless grace and mercy that's in my life. You are my constant reminder that God can and will do amazingly above and beyond what my mind has the ability to imagine. Therefore, I continue to imagine great things. Thank you both.

To my immediate family, my sister Dr. Jasmin Brown, my brothers Terrence and Alan Brown, thank you all so much. I am so blessed to have family that has always supported and believed in my endeavors. I recognize that I have such a long way to go, but I want to assure you that I am on my way. Thank you.

To my good friends and supporters, thank you for sticking with me through the good, the bad and those unclear moments. We are not finish yet and the best is yet to come. Thank you.

Lastly, to all the individuals of my past with whom I have had unfavorable encounters, thank you. I am thankful for the experience and times I shared with you because it was those overwhelmingly dark and perplexed moments that forced me to examine my life with such passion and drive. The agonizing discomfort propelled me to search internally for my own solution to the repetitive and redundant cycle I often found myself in. With much developed tenacity and vigor, I had to create a plan to change my life pattern. Thus, I've learned to love and trust myself which allowed me to discover this phenomenal process that has transformed my life. I am now determined to share this principle with the world via this book. Thank you!

To all my future friends, readers and supporters, thank you from the core of my heart.

Thank you